Synonyms
for (OTHER) Bodies

Synonyms for (OTHER) Bodies

Poems by

Daryl Sznyter

NYQ Books™

The New York Quarterly Foundation, Inc.
New York, New York

NYQ Books™ is an imprint of The New York Quarterly Foundation, Inc.

The New York Quarterly Foundation, Inc.
P. O. Box 2015
Old Chelsea Station
New York, NY 10113

www.nyq.org

First Edition

Set in New Baskerville

Layout and Design by Raymond P. Hammond

Front and Back Cover Illustrations by Barry Barosky

Author Photograph by George Schirra

Library of Congress Control Number: 2018930053

ISBN: 978-1-63045-055-7

for my mom and dad, who gave me this body,
my brother who lectured me on the science behind it,
and my grandma, who showed me what it's capable of

Contents

Me

Acknowledgements

My infinite gratitude goes out to everyone who made this book possible, some of whom may know it, and others who'd be surprised at the magnitude of their impact.

First I'd like to thank NYQ Books and Raymond Hammond for thinking what I have to say is interesting enough to attach NYQ's name to it. Thanks to Barry Barosky for attaching a striking visual to my words. (Couldn't have said it better myself!) Thank you to George Schirra, for making me look like a supermodel in my author picture, and for a friendship brighter and fiercer than a Louboutin's red sole. Sincerest appreciation to Amanda Bradley, Elaine Equi, and John Struloeff for your blurbs. I'm truly blessed to have the kind words of people I respect so highly on the back cover.

Special thanks also to the editors of the following magazines and anthologies where various individual poems first appeared: *The American Journal of Poetry, American Writers Review, Artemis Journal, Belletrist, Best American Poetry Blog, Bluestem Magazine, Bop Dead City, The Broke Bohemian, Clockhouse, Eunoia Review, The Flexible Persona, Folio, Freshwater Literary Journal, Gravel, Malevolent Soap, Mercurial Noodle: Theories of HER Anthology, Noble/Gas Qtrly, Panoply, Phoebe, Really System, Third Wednesday, WomenArts Quarterly,* and *Word Fountain.*

A huge thank you to my mom, Sharon Sznyter, for encouraging my love of the written word even when others questioned its profitability; to my father, Wallace Sznyter, for advocating self-expression at all costs (sometimes to the point of distress); to my brother, Scott Sznyter, for being one of my biggest fans and providing me with a plethora of interesting facts on a variety of different subjects, some of which are included in these pages; to my grandmother, Sophie Zbylicki, whose often not-so-gentle guidance taught me to believe in myself enough not to take anyone else's baloney; and to my uncle, Robert Zbylicki, for introducing me to some of my all-time favorite books and for teaching me the finer points of grammar on our morning commutes so that I might purposefully break every rule in a book such as this.

Thank you to Michael Sulima for a truly unique bond more powerful than our vestigial Catholic guilt. Thanks to the makeshift Women Writers Group for being the first to hear many of these poems. To my professors, teachers, and instructors—I will never stop being amazed at the faith and encouragement you've given me over the years, and my appreciation for the knowledge you've imparted is never-ending.

To everyone who ever attended one of my poetry readings and to those who approached me afterwards to wrap me in their shared experiences—I love you with more intensity than I could ever put into words.

Last but not least, my immeasurable thanks and adoration go to Brian Fanelli for his unconditional love and confidence in my writing. Without him, this manuscript would be nothing more than a bunch of crumpled papers stuffed in our junk drawer.

The Virgin to Gabriel

enter my room   *lightly*
muddy   *footprints on a wooden floor*
fill me i'm   *frigid*
furnace   *didn't kick in tonight*
none of that   *hand-holding*
flower   *fire hard play*
take me   *raw*
wear   *out my knees*
bruise my soft   *places*
i'd   *rather watch you*
do it than do it to   *myself*
don't   *clean up*
your mess   *leave*
go   *bother god*

Me

_____

synonyms for (other) bodies

i am fat & i am invisible
i go out to eat in groups
& the waitress always
seems to forget my food
it takes me two rounds
to get a beer & after four
we go because everybody
is looking at me because
nobody is looking at me
because i already paid i hit
up the gym in all black
a big black marble i am
invisible big muscled men
lift weights next to me
& i am in their space
their space i move back
with every lunge & i
am in their space & i
move back with every
bicep curl & i am in their
space they hug my space
with their piney sweat
until i have nowhere else
to go but out on my way
out somebody says girls
of my stature will never
outrun their problems i
run fast until i'm origami
& bones i fold in i fold
in i can use my wrists
as scissors i cut my hair
to expose the elegance
of my cheeks i leave
my hair on the floors
of coffee shops & they
still forget my coffee

& i still pay so now
i only drink water
& scrape the glass
with my thinning teeth
& still i am invisible
i accentuate those
striations under my
ribcage i carve out
the meat & feed my
loved ones & still i am
invisible i raise my hand
to ask a question & i am
invisible i interrupt & i am
rude one day i spoke into
silence until my tongue
lit on fire when i paused
for water somebody else
stood up to pawn off my
story & the audience went
wild

My Mother's Yellow Dress

The perfect dress.　　　　My mother's dress.　　　　　　I envy the dress.

　　Pretty yellow dress.　I.　Pretty.　Mother.　　My mother hanging the dress.

My mother.　　　　　　　　　　Hanging.　　　　　　　Dress.

　　My mother hanging in the dress.　I.　Envy.　　I envy hanging.

I envy hanging the dress.　　　　　　　　I envy hanging in the dress.

　　　I envy hanging my mother in the dress.

I envy my mother.　I.　The.　I.　Perfect.　Hanging.　Yellow.　Yellow dress.　Yes.

My Grandma Battles the Loch Ness Monster

My grandma used to wash my hair
like it was fine china. Her apron an ammo
belt slung low on her hips, she'd bend me
over the basin, holding me by the nape
of my neck with hands so cold I swore
they were stones at the bottom of a river.
Only she saw the beauty in those flat,
dishwater brown knots I stuck in my mouth
and sucked on when I was nervous.
Only she was brave enough to test the water
on her own flesh first, patient enough to hold
the showerhead at the precise angle to keep
shampoo out of my eyes and conditioner
rolling off my forehead like mercury.
Her pruned fingers, a comb with the finest
teeth, untangled strand by strand like unraveling
a dreamcatcher. Sometimes she held the blow dryer
to my scalp for too long, but I persevered
as the women before me did. At the end,
she'd restrain my bangs with a butterfly clip,
exposing my hairline like a crack in pavement.

bad girl

my first nun told me i'm bad
told me i can't give away my body
but i am the architect of my body
tell me i can't give it away
& i will show you my building
i will show you the bricks of my bones
stucco of my skin
& misplaced cigarette mouth
busted out windows all over me sister
that christ man might be bread
but this body is ash & even as ash
i am promiscuous
even your father sticks his thumb in me
once a year & shares me
with his whole congregation

the largest scab in my life

was from the time i cut my legs into ribbons because i thought i was pregnant & catholic school made me afraid of abortions i still have it saved in a sandwich bag because it's so impressive i pulled up to my former place of work to pick up my girlfriend who quit that night & no i wouldn't go to the hospital why didn't i go to the hospital because they would never let me out of the hospital anyway & all it takes to wake me up is jumper cables & i have those in the trunk of my car peeling it off was more therapeutic than what we're doing anyway at that time i was having too much sex & then i wasn't having enough sex & then i wasn't having the right kind of sex & then sex became painful like that kathy acker book blood & guts in high school like the women in all the books i read should've had that abortion maybe it would have prepped me yeah i smoked a lot of weed back then but i was already mad at that point & i didn't want to come home to another disappointment so i slept over her house that night i was in love with her at that time i'm still in love with her but it's more like the love a lion has for its cub we take turns being the lion and the cub now i'm in goo goo gaga love with the most rational person i know i know you'll say that suits me but i still crave the good ol' mutilation doesn't your blood get lonely & want someone to play with why won't i do it because he'd check me she'd check me & you don't hurt people you love you fill them with worry but you never ever hurt them you ask me if i need to go to the hospital now & i mean well i'd need to get sick again first what do you mean who saves their scabs?

sometimes it's like i'm speaking to an empty room

somewhere feelings are the color of salt   somewhere twilight isn't so greedy
          somewhere i smash dishes against the wall
                              i drown out the noise of violent bodies
somewhere feels like home   feels like heaven
        i could call you without repercussions   somewhere i love myself
somewhere my parents aren't divorced   somewhere i'm not divorced from myself
        somewhere the sound of lions making love   the smell of daffodils
the taste of fresh macaroons   my backpack is always half empty
                    the train is just arriving
                              somewhere words fall from my lips like smoke
somewhere i feel like writing   somewhere everyone is naked without speaking
somewhere there is speaking without pressure   somewhere books are free
            we are free   trees grow without oxygen
          somewhere we grow without questioning it
somewhere the planet is uninhabitable somewhere we dance a million ballets

When I said my very body was a political act

I meant the viragos of my being glows
back at me from a flat screen at the gym

and here I am stumbling on the treadmill,
the hips of my foremothers swiveling in poor

form, thinking to myself no wonder I'm arthritic.
A child somewhere finds a bomb in his shoe

and I've long ago stopped thinking my money
will help him. Please give. Please give. These

words mean nothing anymore. Burnt flesh means
nothing if it doesn't grow in my stomach. Nothing

grows in my stomach. The newswoman smiles
through clenched teeth in between stories of one

shooting and then another because she was told smiles
boost ratings. Her male counterpart laughs nervously

and on the next screen a different station raves
about carb-free pizza. The pizza looks disgusting

but I know you can trick yourself into thinking
anything is delicious. For example, I once only ate

things that passed through me undigested, dreaming
cotton balls were ice cream, screaming as they sliced

through me, running cracked finger pads over ascetic
ribs. I was a dancer. A child on one of the screens dances.

She is from a different country. Blind, deaf, and mute,
she dances. Her parents say she is a miracle. Unhearing,

she dances. And through her is how I remember.

i skip work for adult ballet class

i got back confusing ½ days
with ½ hrs. i got back that bobble-

head neck, those always freshly-
cried doll eyes. i got back dermatillo-

mania & medicationless mania. trichotillo-

mania & high school breasts. i got back hips
my father was proud of & collar bones

my mom just called bones. i lost sleep.
no need to sleep. no desire. no. desire.

i got back bipolar, like the weather—

except not. i got back mirrors, so many
mirrors. i got back dressing in darkness.

i lost 50 lbs. i got back perfect splits. dead-
on pirouettes, back curled towards an unseen

ceiling like an open jewelry box. i got a spine.

i lost 50 lbs. i got a big forehead.
i got back headaches from hair pulled

too tight. i got back my old scratched Bach
cds. i got back Bach. i got back music. i lost

words i lost words i lost words i lost words i lost—
i got back music. i got—

My Grandma Asks Me Why I Pierced My Nose

I never liked my nose. Sometimes it feels good to be
masochistic. Stick a needle in it and people are afraid of you.

I can always remove the metal if for some reason
I learn to adore it. Remember when you told me my lips

would swell if I kissed a boy before my eighteenth birthday?
Did you not notice how they chap in winter? How blood bursts

from them like a water bucket overflowing? This hoop will distract
from that. I will make you proud. It is impossible

to go through life without knowing what a mirror is.
Everybody needs a focal point. This metal is what my face

has always been missing. It distracts from my asymmetry.
How can you tell me you don't understand

when your own stretched holes droop in your ears,
a reminder of the two lead weights that balanced

your head like a scale for many, many years?

Punk Shows with You

I go for the names: The Descendants, Subhumans,
Mischief Brew—my ancestral nomenclatures. We stand
in the back, holding hands through crossed arms. Nodding
our heads in acknowledgement of the brass cymbals banging loud
enough to summon seizures. I laugh as a man with a dissected
pig on his shirt punches a skinny kid in the face, drawing blood
from his lip, sweat wilting both of their superglued liberty spikes.
You explain that this is their dance, that the hair is part
of their subculture the way ballet buns are part of mine.
When I'm with you, it doesn't matter that my magnolia
sundress makes me a target for riot-grrl ridicule
because I know you would shield me from wind-milling arms
and machete-sharpened fingernails. I still don't understand
the difference between genres and am not certain I really
want to. At the end of the show, we drive home in silence
because any words would garble like water in our ears.
We finish the night in bed, embracing each other despite
the stench of our flesh. You curl around me like a hook
and smile into my hair, convincing me that even anarchy
can be tender.

first time in a bikini since 16

& baby i still got it
my partner asks me not to speak
while he lathers me with sunscreen
can't concentrate on 2 things
at the same time

my skin outshines
the rhinestones on my sunglasses
my bones are a classic car too precious
to drive 'til some rich chick's daddy
buys me for her birthday

the woman behind me is having a baby
a photographer holds a camera
to her smile
the nylon of her skirted navy one-piece
stretches so far i could hear it

her husband steps in seagull shit
trying not to touch me
she follows me to the restroom
slams the toilet seat down in the next stall
to threaten me

we wash our hands together
the best & worst thing about beach
bathrooms is the lack of mirrors
& the long walk back
through hot heavy sand

on my way i think of
the last time i wore this bikini
i was 16 & a virgin
i was so small it fell
right off me.

summer prophecy

the clouds are not three
dimensional the sky is not a picture
book home is our version of utopia something
that will never exist because to desire
is to desire there is a reason people
don't follow their dreams in the end to desire
is more satisfying than anything one can accomplish
the intangible summons the hair on our arms
and i think the weather is obsessed with me
my mouth summons moisture summons
floods thunders ice into water
the sun reflects weather advisories off my breasts
that never come to fruition
raises boils on my skin knows
people ache for what they are most afraid of
people ache for me strangers deify me rub me
pilgrimage on the map of my scars chant
my leper my leper singing and singing
celebrating like i'm not even there

Strawberry Picking Season

I wish you spoke about me the way you talk
about pies at the farmer's market.

You disapprove of curse words yet can't stop
yourself from moaning *fuck, they're so good.*

Can't the lovingness of my ribcage pressed against
yours parallel the warmth of a broken lattice?

When my arms move around you and in you
and through you, leaving you sticky with sweat,

does it evoke the same emotion as jam dribbling
down your chin on a humid day, staining your white

T-shirt with sin? I notice the unexpected smile
break your lips when you cut the first slice.

If only your face flushed like that
in response to my naked flesh.

maybe i should fill my poems with flowers

i write poetry because no one else will have
me you point out the neighbor's flowers
every time we pass his house he has no grass but the rose
bushes are still blooming in autumn only pink things in autumn

like the alien way someone calls your name
when they are calling a stranger you feel dumb for snapping

back your neck remember the way bloodlines curl around pipes
in winter the way i'm afraid to turn up the heat when you're
sleeping

stare at your picture of frankenstein on the wall thinking
he's the closest thing you have to another woman the cat

sleeps on my hip bones comforted by sharp things the windows
go sodden you blot away mold touch the veins at my throat
when summer shines them bridal their fragile chem
trails belie the huh of the words that spill out of them

God Doesn't Care about Global Warming

I wonder if you're thinking about how
you used to walk this trail with your ex,
coffee in one hand, the other wrapped
around her waist. I'm almost glad for
global warming. For the way the leaves
are more chartreuse than golden or red.
For the way they seem to hit the ground
green and transform for us and us alone.
If you could read my mind, you would
tell me to stop being so narcissistic.
White moths ghost around us like halos
and dandelions still won't shed their seeds
without a child's lips. I wish you'd walk
slower so I could tiptoe over the leaves.
Why can't we let them die in peace?
Nothing can ruin this for me. Not
the sewage plant we'll pass on the way
back. Not the metal clang of a car
accident just beyond the foliage.
Not even the idea that the leaves
will continue to fall no matter what color
they are. That soon snowflakes will replace
them. I don't mind stocking up on balm
to keep my lips smooth for you, pressing
myself against you to stop the shakes.
Thanking my mother profusely for the gloves
she got me last Christmas, the red leather
that will soon save my stubborn hands
as they clutch an iced coffee,
even in winter.

Red Roses on Valentine's Day

valentine's day is my favorite holiday even when i'm alone almost everything is lust red almost everything roses you gave me roses but they weren't red enough brown isn't a type of red & red wine runs too smooth down my red palate i don't like the games you play with red

this year i have my period but i don't mind menstruating because i feel red inside (redder than usual) i sometimes think about smearing the red on the walls on your face on the door handle i can't remember the last time i opened the door for myself when i'm red i want everyone else to be red too is that so much to ask to feel red is to feel relief is to feel a flood inside

boys bleed red too when they're babies but you've never been circumcised in fact i'm not sure you've ever bled at all you must have been saving your red for me me with my red lips and red fingernails even my hair was red once

i'll get you out of my bloodstream one day do you know there are kids who have this red disease where they want to eat their own hands that's a real dedication to red i wish i had that kind of dedication i bet if i could cry my tears would be red i bet if i could bleed my blood would be blue that's why i choose not to let you cut me open

when i was with you i used to listen for red sirens in the distance their red is angry but i stopped listening because i'm not so mad anymore instead i notice the red-winged angels you probably call them cardinals anyway now i listen for their beautiful red songs singing red red i bleed my soul in red noisy voices in a crowded room

Our First Fight

you caught my hair
in my zipper
zipping up my coat
for me

back then
i didn't know you
well enough
to pick up on your
impatience

and you didn't know me
well enough to know
i'd find it condescending

so you thought
you were protecting
me and i thought
you were hurting me

but neither of us
said a word that day
and now it's fall
again

and the zipper
on this coat
doesn't even
work anymore.

When People Ask Me Where I Grew Up

When I lived in California, locals used to tell me they were surprised
at my lack of a Pennsylvania accent. Question: How many words
in the dictionary mean scorn or censure? Answer: I used to know but I forgot
or maybe I lost count. Question: How many words are in the English
language? Answer: There is no sensible answer. Language is subjective.
Does sand in the hair weigh down your syllables? My lungs seize
up in negative weather. Yes, like snow in spring. Like dying
when only yesterday you recovered your happiness. My vocal
cords clutch their arm holes when my elders enter the room.
That doesn't mean I imitate my parents. We all morph enunciation
to fit in with our culture. We all want to fit into the place we call home.

Small-Town Famous

I'll never make it in this town
because I'm the girl who wears glittered
Mary Janes to breakfast. The one
with the cool-girl hair that enamors
children and scares their mothers.
I have less hair than some men I know
and that, too, scares their mothers. I walk
up to strangers who look like friends
who think I'm a friend. I don't have
friends. I don't yank my dress
down my thighs when it rides
up in public. My body is flat
and soft like a well-oiled rifle,
but these men are hunters
and damn good at it too.
My papa taught me how to load
a gun, but they're quicker
and they know it.
I run from them like a greased-up pig.
I don't wear camouflage.
I don't listen to country music.
I don't have any pictures of me
with fish bigger than my arm span.
I only feel naked when I'm not
wearing lipstick. I take notes in my phone
in crowded rooms and guard them
like mysterious lovers. I go braless
in sun dresses. I never have a quick
enough tongue when teenage boys honk
their horns at me but I will Carrie
Underwood the fuck out of their Jeeps
by moonlight. I will spit in the dirt
and write my name in it. I think books
are the best dinner dates. I think men
and women are equally beautiful,
and I don't think that makes me a bad

person. I am not a commodity and that makes me a bad person. I steal their newspapers some mornings, and if they knew it was me they'd say that makes me a really, really bad person.

Perfume

I want you to breathe me in like our grandfathers
ate coal dust. Think of me when you cook with vanilla.
Inhale when you pass the neighbor's rosebush
on the way to your car in the morning. Find me in strangers—
men and women—and want to French them in dark hallways
like the two leads in one of those made-for-TV detective movies.
Look forward to opening the bedroom door after work
to find me in my pajamas, scented fresh out of the shower.
Press your head to my chest and go slack in the framework
of my arms as I ask you about your day. Hold my hand
as we read together, letting go only to turn the pages,
catching a whiff fanned up by the words on paper.

Bettie Page in Our Kitchen

If I have to sleep under twelve Universal Monsters
posters, then god damn it, Bettie Page will hang
in our kitchen. Her cigarette needs to smolder over
your eggs and juice, reminding you of every reason
I truncate my words like naughty pictures so you'll
want to hump me before we go to work.
You've captured the monster's bride at six
different angles and she didn't even like him.
At least with Bettie, you know what you're getting.
I gape at the small of your back when you can't see
me, wear bullet bras when you're away. I tilt my pelvis
to the gods when you're asleep on the couch.
Practice my touch on myself. Maybe I'm the one
you should be afraid to introduce to your mom.
Like Dracula, I fantasize about my teeth on your neck.
I'm also into bondage.

Chantelle 1745 D 34

perhaps the most
emollient thing
to ever grace the stiff
colanders of my
breasts to bring
on the grand
loquaciousness
i've only ever seen
those shy tongues
dare to exhibit
at the piercing
of my nipples
and even those poor
newborns are not
yet rehabilitated
chantilly swirls
oh victorian
damsels who
knew an overcast
taupe could make
a mirror of my sparse
wet flourlike skin
almost free of last
summer's muddy
tan an accident
it never asked for
D 34 means france
values cup over
band child over
mother 1745
means merci
its eponym rooted
in the wheeze
of lungs free
from constriction
with light blinked
on after sleeping
well past all alarms
merci they would
squeal *i aver i aver!*

IUD Insertion

& here I am

sundress folded back at the hips
panties scrunched to ankles
knees knocking together
along with the radio
shaky hands wound up & icy
with the biting shame
of a catholic school spanking
or a period in khaki pants
or virginity
or an std

& here he is

scent of anesthetic & coffee
gloved hands
rubber smoother & thicker
than the blood in my womb
ready to hollow me out & insert
a boomerang on a string
he calls our indiscretions
doin' the wild thang
opens me up like a painting
& I scream

& there you are

making yourself small in the corner
white knight to my wasted ovaries
paler & sicker than my tissue
paper blanket
a face miraculously empty
of questions
you slide me from the table
as soon as he lets you
& ask the nurse for a napkin
to wipe my thighs

41

In Celebration of My Uterus

after Anne Sexton

Everyone in me is lost.
They babble.
They inked their words
on your lips once.
Now they are illegible.
They sucked up the worms
they heaved on you once.
Now they are losing
their feathers.

I pluck their feathers.

Their feathers are gray
all over the floor.
You kill them
all over the floor.
You are red
all over the floor.
You are a closed
screen and an open
door.

Learning to Dance

I always knew.
I've been swingin'
longer than my sweat's
been stinking up men's sheets.
My aunt almost named me
Tango and my gram,
Queen of Polka, agreed.
But my momma, still looking
for a man under her own skin,
named me something
I'd be forced to learn.

The best way to waltz
is with an empty space for a face
and the body of a coat hanger.
On a sunny day in a pencil dress,
I can be foxy. Sure, tight Nylon
sometimes makes words irrelevant,
but don't think for a minute
She's boxing me in. This fox
doesn't trot. She soars. She spins.

I've been fat. I've been thin.
The best ballerinas are the ones
flat as stamps. We make unsuspecting
men find Jesus and carry us in boxes,
dropping pretty things at our feet
for as long as we pirouette
in one place.

My momma gave me a man's name
so when I lead, others follow.

I am the Voodoo Queen

Marie Laveau has nothing on me.
I make art with strands
of our hair on shower walls.
You'll love me forever
whether you want to
or not. We don't need
any 30-dollar potions.
Make an altar
for your crystals
and expose them
during the supermoon.
I can align your chakras
with the warmth
of my hands,
cleanse you with
rose oil on my breath.
If you ever leave
I will stick you
with pins
but I love you
I love you
so I have no choice
but to teach you
to protect yourself
from me.
I can't be burned
in the erotic ways
of myth.
You alone can
undo what is already done.
You alone will be privy
to my charm.
One day there will be
a museum in our names.
Statues of us will wear diadems.
Tourists will speculate
if our eyes are made of emeralds
and children will swear that we
follow them at all times.

We

The World Needs Angry Women

We are street performers on empty
streets. We are blisters. We walk over broken glass
and steaming pavement. We feed our sweat
to plants. We give up
our spirits but we can't get out of them.
Give us babies or we will die.
We are vinyl, leather, fabric of unknown origin—
easily scuffed yet fetishized,
handed down from generation to generation.
Always presenting.
It is not through lack of finesse that you feel
the scrape of our teeth
like lead, like California tap water
straight from a rusty faucet.
We chew our tongues to pills.
We do not speak. We swallow.
Swallow you whole like a purge
because we are active.
Because we are proud.
Because our wombs are made of rubber.
We are sunlight leaking
through bony shoulders.
Our bare chests prick
your eyes like burrs.
We hang from your neck, public
as a jewel yet hidden as a piercing.
If you love us, you will let us step on your face
with boots, not heels—stop thinking
about penetration.
If you love us, be our victory
over every unwanted advance.
If you love us, you will lap
up the salt beneath our feet.

Washington Tulips

after Eileen Myles

we are those women
disappointing
our fathers
we make pink ugly
we shut the sky
off like a smashed light-
bulb we are the brown
spots melting the snow
earth that fools
with its tenderness
stick a shovel in us
and we will resist
with smiles so beautiful
and uncomfortable

Skin Cell

because she is more than
the sum of her parts
because she doesn't answer
prayers
because you can't trust her
to be there in the morning
because she's not
a beer bottle
on your nightstand
because her pores
are grains of sand
because she is an hourglass
in the bathtub
because the water
is getting icy
look at her face
just below the ice
just behind the mirror
just behind
the television screen
in your mind
because you keep hitting
rewind because
no matter how hard you hit
that screen
it's not going to break
because there are two
kinds of cells
the ones you're made of
and the ones
you end up in
because her brother
is the biologist
in the family
because she uses
her words

to build a moat
around her
because they kept
walking toward her
when she asked them
to stop.

The Sex Talk

When my father tried to tell me
about sex, he said,

women
are like pomegranates—
nobody
really knows how to eat you.

if we swallow your seeds
will you grow in our bellies?

When my mother tried to tell me
about sex, she said,

women
are like avocados—
nobody
really knows when we're ripe.

if they wait too long,
you will rot.

How easy it is to rot.

Two Ways to Divide an English Muffin

i.

Longing is the shine of a knife
and you've been on that gluten-
free kick for way too long. Get
out your measuring tape and find
the perfect median. Cut. Lick
the crumbs from the cutting
board. Make sure you sanitize
it first.

ii.

Waiting is overrated. Dig those
untrimmed nails into its sides
and rip it in half. Toast it. You
like it a little overdone but not
black. Sometimes you pop it out
too soon. Sometimes you get so
angry with hunger you couldn't
hold back if you wanted to.

Two Ways to Put on Stockings

i.

Be the silhouette of a mud flap girl.
Sink into that indentation in your mattress.
Slide them up gently like rising bread.
Pull the crotch as taut as black nylon
will allow. Curl your feet into meat hooks.

ii.

Jump up and down until your rattling breasts
complain. Jive your hips. Yank them over your
thighs like a no-good child. Give your varicose
veins a story. Always play music you can pop
your pelvis to. Rejoice in that thinly veiled skin.

at the laundromat

we tell time by the flickering
of fluorescent light bulbs. all the wicked
are offered a moment's reprieve—
one moment, every eighteen minutes
on the dot. clothes always come out gray
& never quite dry & usually the people
scare me so that i'm afraid to read
the book on my lap in case their thoughts
turn into the words on the page
& jump off & down into my own throat
& then they will know that sometimes
i steal their detergent when they're not looking
& i will know if they've fantasized
about me in my pastel panties
with the disgraceful bloodstains
on the cotton crotch.

moon cycle

mine usually comes
when the moon is still shaped
phallic maybe that's why i
thought it was over this morning
and left your sheets vandalized
with menses like children
spray-painting storefronts
if i had noticed what i had become
i wouldn't have bothered
to clean your skin with mine

anything can look virginal
if you want it to like cleaning
up a crime scene
see
nothing to see here

women have spent eternities
struggling to speak in tongues
but we still reach into our purses
during dinner and make a beeline
for the bathroom, tampon shoved
up our sleeves, that distinct crinkle
of plastic wrapping trapping us
like animals rustling in the bush
when all they want to do is hide
believe me we want to hide

but our only other alternative
is to sit in our own blood.

what you learn when you only speak when spoken to

a dress is not a dress unless the kneecaps
have an agenda. nobody notices a new hair-

cut unless it exposes the neck. the face is invisible
until it is painted on. the little boy at the park

usurps his sister. if you don't believe it, ask
for her name. she is a board game with flexible

instructions. we are multiple choice questions
answered *all of the above.*

our mothers sent us to charm school to learn
how to act but never raised our brothers

to be ashamed of their erections.

sirens

your laws
reach the ends
of us in the   strangest
ways, like eels
making their way
through our stomachs
emerging from our   mouths
like the pearls
you want to stick   inside
of us, forming
our brand-
new slithering   tongues.
no is at their steely
beginnings.
we, the   iconoclasts
will blaspheme
your image
until your bones
set to stone.
we will   build
your wall
with you
and smash
it with the tiniest
chisels   crack
into you slowly
with our exquisite
teeth.

New York Love Poem

Traffic is the best part.
The horns wake me at 6 am
to keep me humble,
reminding me of my narrow
escape from being ordinary.
On my way to class
at the most expensive art school
in the city, a man with blood
on his shirt offers me coke
and I ask him if it is flour
and is it organic
and will it leaven my bread?
In Union Square, a man
with no arms or legs
moves a skateboard with his
hips and begs me to feed him.
I pretend not to notice
because he is only half a person,
but in reality, I am ashamed
that I work two jobs
and am about to be evicted.
A skeletal man has elephantiasis
of the feet. He makes slippers
out of cardboard boxes
because like Cinderella,
no other shoes will fit.
A man with no face
tells me he is on his way
to the AA meeting on Perry
St. I wonder if he sees me as
a familiar face. I know the building.
I have friends there. Then I see
Jesus with mustard knotted
into his beard. He informs me
only hookers wear yoga pants.
I wonder if I should explain

that I live in the East Village.
On the subway, I think about
my roommate and how she
works overnights at the crustiest
diner in Inglewood. She braves
the two-hour commute home with a
plastic bag over her head to out-crazy
the real crazies. The crazier you want
to seem, the more bags you layer on. I
only acknowledge her genius as a vagrant
tries to steal my backpack. Maybe I'm
not that extraordinary after all.
Maybe my true home is in
the coal miner's town I came from.

Daryl (Race Poem)

He repeated his name three times,
crackling through the white noise
the way knives cut through cheese.
Third time's a charm. Malcolm, I
heard. Like Malcolm X. Like Black
Lives Matter. Like what is wrong
with you. I can't say I know what
it's like to be judged by the color
of my skin or typecast by facial
features or the pigment of my eyes,
but I know what it's like to repeat
my name over and over only to be
called the wrong name anyway.
To have my identity stolen by both
gender and race, my namesake
unfathomable. I can't help but
feel like we possessed each
other. His struggle constant, mine
through distance. In my mind,
I begged him not to hang up
because the next person I called
would think I was a disillusioned
young black man working at a call
center to make ends meet. I want
to hear his story, the way he lives
a life people have only imagined.

They

Advice from Other Women

Section your hair. Straighten it slowly. Too fast and you'll burn it. Don't go over the same spot more than once. Let the ceramic make you beautiful. We don't want singed hair, do we? Scope out groomsmen at weddings. Look for lonely men at coffee shops on holidays. These are the men most likely to want you. Don't cross your legs when you sit. When your brother comes home, sit on the floor. He can see up your skirt. That's uncomfortable for all of us. Let him undress you. At some point it will feel natural for both of you. Watch porn and learn. Tease him, but only if you're going to put out. Don't kill the fantasy. Red lips say fuck me. Pink lips say daddy issues. Ration your time. Sometimes natural is better, but we both know how long that takes. Never be late for a date. Well, maybe fashionably late. Remind him it's all for him. Never kill the fantasy. Don't wear your glasses in public. Never wear your glasses in public. Don't use too much sugar. Don't use too much salt. Butter is your ancestors' secret. It's true what they say about stomachs and hearts. Men have robust hearts. Clog their arteries so they notice you. Ha. That wasn't a joke. Don't forget the bread. He doesn't want to hear about your education. Don't intimidate him. Stop reading books before bedtime, at least until you have children. Give him a marriage timeline. A year of engagement. A year to plan the wedding. Don't let him string you along. Black is slimming. Get perfect winged eyeliner by taping your eyelids. Too much tape will glue them shut. Don't worry if your eyes swell from the adhesive. Allergies are common, but temporary. Never slam the door. Never, ever speak your father's name. Wear a bra. Even when you're sleeping. Even when you're fucking. Fuck in the dark. Never say fuck in public. Don't lift up your slip, honey. I know it's itchy, but you look so cute in that dress and you only have to wear it on Christmas. Buy shoes one size down. Men love a girl with small feet. Tell him you're submissive. Tell him you're a masochist. Guys like that. Never offer to split the check. It's an insult to his masculinity. Never make the first move. Let him open your mouth for the first kiss. Never forget to clean your hair from the tub and makeup from the sink. Rinse any shaving stubble down the drain. Never let him know you shave. Don't kill the fantasy. It's okay to get married more than once. Just make sure none of them ever find out about each other. If a rapist approaches you, tell him you have AIDS. If that doesn't work, piss yourself. If that doesn't work, take it in silence. Or put up a fight. Read his body language. Be what he wants. If he doesn't want you, no one will. Don't end up naked on the Internet. Don't end up pregnant out of wedlock. Offer to split the check. You don't want him to think you're a gold digger, do you? Never be sad. Even if you are, never be sad. Always use protection. Don't be easy. You're a woman, damn it. It's high time you started acting like one. Never say damn it it public.

Acceptance

He being God became man in all things.
He loved the virgin and what did she do with him?
He came in haste and her unborn child-womb leapt with joy.
Dying of hunger, that naked person insisted *you did it to me*.

Smile. I am so used to the dying smile. She is expecting
a daughter. In our own family these are difficult days
for everybody because young parents are a war,
the beginning of impossible peace dying deliberately.

A mother can kill you.
Terrifying, unwedded child—blessing of god!—
We can have a baby whenever we want.
Vowed chastity is a beautiful sentence
and a terrible condition. So I put her in bed
and she said *Thank You*. I could not help but examine
her. Hungry. Dying. Cold. Pain. Grateful love.

Eaten with worms. Animal greatness.
Speak without cursing, angel!
I was unwanted and you did it to me.

We are not real. Touching bombs and sugar.
Extraordinary experience! The joy of sharing.
I want you. Tremendous experience.

Your abundance has hurt you. Home for many.
Spread the woven passion, relived all over again,
difficult to remove. Continual giving.
Give me until it hurts.

Radiating child, unwanted mother. You can go
to heaven for publicity. Purified. Sacrificed.
The unborn child comes out burning.
God bless you!

found poem. source: Mother Teresa's Nobel Prize Acceptance Speech, December 10, 1979

Racing Worms

My earliest memory of my father
is of him teaching me how to gut
a catfish. I didn't like how evisceration
by Swiss Army knife sounded just like
puke hitting pavement, so instead I scooped
two worms out of their container
and dropped them with a pang
onto the boat's metal seats, anticipating
their fall with dirt under my nails.
I wanted them to race. I gave them
names: Wormy and Slim. It might
as well have been ancient Rome.
I cupped my hands around them
so they'd wiggle in a straight line.
The water's mist masked the unforgiving
sun. They shrunk sluggishly enough
for me not to notice. When my dad
found out, he tossed them into
the shimmering lake, wiping red
hands on his white T-shirt.

Learning to Shoot

He took the cheap one for himself,
the one you had to aim a few feet
to the right if you wanted to hit
your target. He moved it
as an extension of his own body,
talking about men in bars flashing
them at each other like wallets,
often with no intention to shoot.

He had a license to carry,
but the gun remained in a safe
in his basement, disassembled
except for times like these
when it was just the two of us,
deep in the woods behind
my childhood home.

If he ever pulled a gun on somebody,
he was going to use it, he said,
proving his point by toppling our row
of meticulously arranged coffee tins,
running to rearrange them
as I prepared to do the same.

I had the better one, the one that practically
aimed itself. Smaller and quieter, so light
in my hand I was convinced it would float
had I tossed it over my shoulder.

I struggled to fit the ammo in the chamber.
Until that day, I'd only seen guns in movies.
The movies, like my father, make it look easy—
one swift movement with strong hands
and a hollow click.

To My Father, Who Says My Body Hasn't Spawned a Political Movement

Tell that to the man who calls me a cunt in front of a gaggle of children crossing the street between school and church. I see the way distraction mounts his face, that mustard seed of hope twitching under his eyelids for a strong breeze or slipped safety pin to expose the white light under those plaid skirts. You may think this is an isolated incident, but it is a regular part of my morning commute. He lives on my street. I don't know which house is his, but he knows which one is mine. I have a flashlight on my keychain for the 10-foot walk from my car to the back door. He circles the block in that big black pickup after even the bars are empty, the night's spilled booze coagulating on tile floors. He serenades our block with country music and the snarl of his souped-up exhaust, hocks wads of Skoal into flowerbeds. He was always this angry, but he just recently learned how to release his venom into an open wound. Now emboldened, he keeps that truck freshly-washed so that every time he runs me off the road, I'm left to fixate on the shine of the only pure thing he owns, the way water bullets sweat down its black body like tears.

Acknowledgement

My mother was always beautiful in a way I'll never be.
Coiled lashes. Rose-in-snow cheeks.
Gold sequined dresses that blinked at you under chandeliers.
Even on Sundays, she was spectacular, sauntering
to church in her modest pumps, a flash of calf
sparking fire under priests' holy robes.
She communicated her love of diamonds
through her fingernails.
Whether oval and salty like almonds
or slender and sharp as a night worker's heels,
they shone in a way that demanded you adorn
the fingers that held them,
and quickly at that or you'd lose the chance.
She had that allure of a woman who needed no one,
but tricked herself into thinking her vocation
was somewhere between sacrifice and being seen.
A glitch in God's plan, that's what they called her.
And me? A mockingbird with no feathers.

Pennsylvania Dress Factory

She was hired to mass produce
when mass production was still new.
At first she sewed like she was slipping
her entire life through the head of the needle
and stood stiff as a soldier
while women around her churned out
a hundred dresses to her ten,
not realizing that they were the beginning
of an unfamiliar era and that their worth
would become as flimsy as their stitching.
She practiced at home, darning the holes
in her family's shreds until her hands
moved like bullets sealed with a kiss.
Day by day, she moved up the line
until she earned her place of honor
by the only window in the factory
where the sun scorched her skin
and the noise dulled her senses.
She wanted to make it her home
until her body became a spool of yarn
that she no longer knew how to manipulate.
The factory burnt down a few years
after she left, her lips the only
fabric that didn't turn to ash.

Why Winter Reminds Me of Violence

When I was three, I lost my boot in a blizzard.
For my mom it was like losing me, her only daughter.
But I had another boot and she had another child—
my brother. And he had both boots. And then there was
my father, who had both boots and couldn't tell the difference
between my brother and me because my mom dressed us
in identical snowsuits. And then there were our neighbors
and their front porch, swept free of snow and decorated
with six pairs of boots in various sizes.

My father would've snatched me a boot if my mom
and brother weren't around, but they were around
so he spent the day digging holes in the yard while my brother
built snow people and I watched from behind a window
in the kitchen and my mother mopped the floor nobody
ever walked on with bare feet and our Christmas decorations
stayed up that year until the first day of spring.

Why We Threw Peanuts at the Family in Front of Us at the Circus

Did we hate them for holding hands because nobody held ours?
Was it because her mother drank too much?
Because my father worked too much?
Was it because a nun told our grandmas we'd end up in jail?
Was it because they were smiling?

Was it because our breasts were emerging and our nipples were angry?
Were we angry because the boys in our class wanted to eat us like peaches?
Were we angry because anatomy was the sixth-grade science?
Was it because we had no clue how to manipulate our bodies?
Did we hate their mother because she was pretty?

Was it because girls like us would never walk tightropes?
Were we mad our parents wouldn't buy us an elephant ride?
Were we mad our parents wouldn't buy us an elephant?
Was it because we looked like clowns?
Because we had no clue how to apply the makeup we stole from Family Dollar?
Because we applied ourselves in school but nobody noticed?
Did we just want them to notice us?

Was it because straight As don't matter when you're not a good girl?
Was it because their kids had books and we had nothing to hide behind?
Was it an attempt to mitigate our social anxieties?
Did we want new friends?

Did we hate them because they had cotton candy and we didn't?
Did we hate them because the peanuts we threw at them were from the floor?
Were we hungry?
Bored?

Did we forget who we were, or not notice the difference?
Was our whiteness a hard candy melting in our pockets?
Was their blackness an ink pen exploding in our pockets?

Where did we learn it?

Did we teach it to ourselves?
Did we not know better?

Did anybody really mean it when they made us apologize?
Did we? Apologize, I mean.
Did we apologize?

Tutu Girl at a Rock Concert

a mother and daughter hold hands and imitate
the singer from the back row. the daughter wears
a tutu in the crowded stadium & nobody hurts her.

if all mothers let their daughters
wear tutus on the swarming streets
of cities, we'd all turn out a little less

like them & maybe that's something
to aim for. i consider my own mom,
& the make-pretend treasure

chests she'd gift me for my birthday,
enticing me with the idea that i really could be
a princess, but only behind dusty curtains,

hidden from our neighbor
& his binoculars. i'd grow up the way
i remember her then: breaking,

breaking up, breaking, always speaking
as someone hearing her voice through a tape
recorder for the first time, suffocating

in her car outside the grocery store,
unable to shake the warble
of the way she sounds to others.

how giddy the little girl in the tutu
must feel to sing & shake her rump,
unaware of anything outside

the swish of tulle against
her thighs & the squeeze
of her mother's hand.

Table Manners

Important something-or-other
On first date
With college woman
And her daughter
College woman pretends
To answer emails
Makes clicking noises
With her assembly line
Acrylic nails
Crystals beaming
Sunshine from her fingertips
Daughter pulls a paddle
Brush from her pocket
Strokes long black hair
Over uneaten spaghetti
Important-something-or-other
Lifts a red dress
Places hand on a thigh

Poem for the Skinniest Girl in My Ballet Class

I want

       your shoes when
       the wood is too soft
       to turn on

       your tights after
       your calves carve
       a hole in them

       your leotard strap
       sliding down
       a sweaty collarbone

to be the chocolate
you're willing to starve
the whole day for

How to Fall Asleep and Never Wake Up

The year they discovered my best friend, twenty years old and silent under the heap of her wrecked car, I learned one can sleep forever and never wake up.

That year, her sister, only seventeen, ate magic mushrooms and lost her mind and her brother, fourteen, started running and stopped eating and I didn't eat magic mushrooms but lost my mind anyway as everyone watched my skin, too white to be real, disintegrate before their eyes.

That year I flew to Colorado to see an urn surrounded by pointe shoes. It reminded me more of a wastebasket than the last I would see of the only person I actually spoke to. The cassette that held the music of my entire life was broken. No—not broken—lost. Her sister ran naked through the street a few days later after ingesting a certain fungus at her school's homecoming dance. Most say it was the drugs. Maybe, I said. But I knew exactly what it was.

Her brother started walking with his feet turned out, a remnant of his ballerina sister instilled in him. I ripped the flesh from my arms, hoping to find her somewhere underneath my fingernails until a doctor gave me medicine and I stopped looking under my skin and started playing the game of how long can I sleep before I wake up.

Her sister ended up in an asylum where they gave her the same medicine they gave me. They say she's doing better. What would they say about me? Her brother keeps amassing cross country trophies, winning solely because he imagines running to her. I continue to play the sleeping game, each nap longer than the last, but I always wake up even though I don't always know where I am.

Fourth of July, a Week Before His Death

By the time we grew close, you
had already started posing in pictures,
but in this one you're laughing, a genuine
laugh, with a lazy arm slung around him
and a piece of chicken stuck between
your two front teeth.

New to the group of friends,
I tried to leave the frame. You reached
for me, and as a result, exactly half of me
was captured. One eye, one breast, a glob
of barbeque sauce lingering guiltily
in the left corner of my mouth.

His wicked eyes and shit-eating grin,
that mushroom tattoo on his shoulder.
He told the joke, and even the photographer
must've laughed, hitting the button with shaky
hands, snapping us into a blur, into an image
I'd never remember if not for his sparkler

fizzling crisply in the foreground.

the air is melting

forest light on your skin
clatters
what does a sinkhole
smell like
we are sinking
floating fishes
mold and permutations
i've always been afraid
of the umber in your eyes
you are singing
a song
you were always singing
a song
voice of a dog's
bite
the above world
doesn't know we are
missing
you wouldn't
kiss me
blame it on
the daisies
when you touched
me i became a
patient
waking up
during surgery
i tried to call out
but my own song
wouldn't come

Personal Ad

Me: Lonely, Desperate. Earthworm upended by rain. I am a tombstone.
You: Be the thing that fills it.

I am the dead woman on page 33.
Age 27, died in her home.
Be the cause of death we all make up in our heads.

It's easy to imagine the drowned woman in a lace or linen nightgown,
always white with pockets.

Be the stones in the pockets. We only picture smooth ones.

I am the body found before skin starts to blue,
hair so black against blanched skin I look bald by moonlight.
I look younger than I am.
Be the reality everything about me defies.

I'm so sexless I'm sexy.
Be the wet white fabric that clings to me
like a wedding veil.

My nipples will reach for you, not caught up to the rest of me yet.
I promise to keep us venerated, to keep my shattered teeth in my stomach,
rosary beads to pray on, as long as you scrub the tub the way I'll teach you.
Be the bleach you burned me with. Be the steel you rubbed me with.

I am my legs
and my legs are a one-way highway.
Be the guy on page 12B. Be the eyes of the guy
who discovered a loophole in the law, or a side street.
Be smug, and pernicious.
Be everything I need.

3 Boys in Front of Me at a Wonder Woman Screening

They say she's just like Superman but slower.
They say she takes 20 minutes to catch up to the villains.
They say the villains wait for her, and Dr. Poison isn't really a villain.
They say her outfit is sexy. They say it's too sexy.
They say who needs armor for their tits?
They say who in their right mind would maim those perfect tits?
They say she's okay for a DC movie, but only because the bar is set
    so low already.
They say she's a bossy bitch.
They say her lips are too big and her smile is crooked.
They say she's too tall, and those boots are very unbecoming.
They say her headband is stupid, and so is her ponytail.
They say using love as an excuse for anything is stupid.
They say she should've listened to her mother when she told her
    not to fight.
They say she's no role model for young women.
They say, no matter what she says, pleasure doesn't exist on an
    island without men.
They say their bodies can't exist on an island with no men.
They say their bodies can't exist without men.
They say she's not allowed to exist without men.
They say put away that lasso, woman.
You don't want to know the truth.

to the men who commented on how she squeezed the gas pump

it was at that moment
she wished God had blessed

her with the grace
to make a hurricane out

of her hollowed-out vagina
or the courage to pump

gasoline on their feet
and put out her cigarette

on their shoes either way
she didn't think God would mind

the cleanup

hands on the 6 train at 4:02 am

girl dangles limp wrist
over hanging strap
on subway (handcuffs)

her palms are cut
and bleeding her knees
are cut and bleeding

her lipstick is smeared
in an L-shape (exit wound)
a contact lens is stuck

to her too-pink cheek
in free hand she carries
her heels in limp hand

she carries a rose
with no petals
(she carries a weed)

Under the Skin (2013 film)

A sexy space alien hunts men in Scotland in this extraordinary malarial dream
from Jonathan Glazer.
—*Xan Brooks,* The Guardian

let them sink like water
separating from oil into a void
of their own creation
you are not even human
they don't know what vacuous
means the first thing they see
is your hair your hair
that doesn't even belong to you
then a bra like texturized daisies
panties pasty like pastry and delicious
too let each one think you seduced
them the daises the pastry
won't save you the lumberjack
will still rape you he will burn you
in her skin before the credits
roll like all human things
he is unstoppable

After the Intrusion

she washed apples
over the kitchen
sink

staring at the wall
where a window
should've been

she ignored the bead
of mud sliding
down her thigh

& focused on the water
beads sliding down
her wrists

she focused on
the earth giving up
on the apple

& ignored
the grits clinging
to her starchy blouse

& the mud
caught
at her knee

& the water
caught
at her elbows

for a moment
& then continued
all this under

the window above
the kitchen sink
built too high to see

from its only
purpose to invite
light inside.

Juno's Autopsy

He brings her back
from the scene of a crash
only to force her open like a locket,
struggling to find a home for
the scalpel. Her skin splits at the blade.
Festering fruit.
Its vacuous stench pricks
the nostrils of his audience.
He introduces her to his students,
the white-smocked boys
more interested in the mysteries
of perpetual gestation
than the idea that she might have made
a fine mother.
The supine woman's thighs are pinned shut
in a futile attempt at modesty,
but the boys' search for knowledge
cannot allow her even this one simple dignity.
Latex hands grope at her from every direction,
each one of them scrambling
for a slice of swollen breast or thigh or wing
until with unbent legs and closed eyes
they almost believe her alive.
At last, it is time to show them
her most prized possession,
glaucous and exposed to their egg white eyes,
dangling from its string in her abdomen.
It is only here, submerged in the viscera,
that two flat hearts become relics
and science somehow ceases to exist.

I envy the dead girl

because being dead means unanimous
praise for lying on your back and taking
it.

In Law and Order, a hooker could die
with postmortem spread legs and Pagliacci
lipstick belying her last living act, but Elliot
Stabler won't hesitate to punch someone's
father in the face for calling her one, yet Olivia
was often exempt for being too close to the case.
Lucky for this hooker, her fictional name at least
makes it to the credits. Her friends are less
fortunate, cast as Hooker #1 and Hooker #2.

And then there's Laura Palmer, most famous
dead girl to ever grace public television,
her name alone the source of the show's cult
following. The same way her rape was made
blameless by demonic possession, the show
went off the air the moment she spoke her first
and only words and Cooper head-butted a mirror,
unwilling to acknowledge that her hedonism
was a product of that tight-knit town he was so
close to calling home.

I envy the dead girl because the detective
is always a man. And you can always
count on a man to romanticize a woman
with lips too blue to speak back.

Bald Mountain

you tell me everyone is
going to die and that is life
that is not life i say
life is the saline sweat dripping
from your ears like candle
wax life is the only blueberry
bush on the mountain
that we will walk through
miles of bramble for only to find
that the berries are too ripe
to consume life is the blood dripping
down our legs from the bramble
and the scars i still have from it six months
later life is deer that are not caught
in any headlights it is red birds blue birds
black birds brown birds it is ugly insects
in metamorphosis it is dragonflies it is no wind
today it is pebbles in your shoes
it is water   water   water   water
life is the chiseled names on the resting
place at the top of the mountain
KS, SB, TT + FN together forever
circa 1897

The K Street Prophet

On our way home from Washington,
there is a man standing in the middle
of the road, blocking traffic. I really
wish I could hear what he is yelling
but his words are garbled, whether with
booze or side effects of the wrong
medication, I don't know. I wish I
could stop the car and approach him,
pen and paper in hand, and ask him
to show me what he's fighting for.
Once I understood, we'd make protest
signs and fight for it together. Instead,
I turn to you and say, "There will be
more of this when the government
takes away our healthcare." What
I really mean is that my pills run out
at the end of the week. Instead,
I moan about not having enough
time to see the Smithsonian
and the aching soles of my
blistered feet.

Casino

There's always that old woman with the oxygen
tank, pursed lips wrapped around a cigarette
like a dried poppy, lipstick and spittle
bleeding into the corners of her mouth.
She plays the penny slots, biding her time
until her grandson returns from Afghanistan
with enough money to keep her out of *a* home
and enough time to welcome her into *his* home.
One day he'll return in his veteran's hat and tell her
he's already five weeks retired. He'll take the seat
next to her and none of the fruit will match
up but he'll keep popping in those pennies,
hypnotized by the rasp of her wavering
breath, the clank of coins feeding somebody
else's children—grateful they both found
something bright to hold on to.

Photograph of Joan Didion and Her Daughter

The mourner's delusion of protection
is written all over you, from the way your arms
form a picture frame around her to the special care
you take with your cigarette to make sure her air
is clean in a way you choose for yours not to be.
The lamp behind you blocks the sun like a parasol
and the ornamental blanket on your lap prevents her
smooth thighs from soaking up the stories attached
to yours. She may not belong to you in a literal sense,
but you share the same plaintive eyes. She straddles
your knee defiantly, exposing her palliative powers
to future audiences, knowing you would deny her
participation in whatever way she decides to kill herself.

Hawaiian Spring

What nobody tells you about Hawaii is that spring
is their rainy season. We lived there for four months
before you swore the government was giving you
Brain Cancer. Capital B. Capital C. The infamous black
sand felt like an oil spill under our feet. There was no
sky. I compared mental illness to the Hawaiian hibiscus,
sprouting blooms almost every day and shriveling
up by moonlight. But the clouds obscured the moon.
Looking back, maybe you were right. If we could be
deceived by the myth of paradise, what else is there
that we don't know?

I wanted to Google "How to Kill Yourself"

but I was afraid I'd get a page on "How to Make
a Bomb with Household Materials" and click on it
accidentally or out of curiosity (if only I was a cat!)
and then the government would find me and punish me
by putting me in jail with limited resources or privacy
with which to kill myself and I'm not very creative
(one of the reasons I ended up here in the first place)
so in their own cruel way they'd make things extremely
difficult for me, a non-criminal who has no dogmatic beliefs,
no terrorist ties, not a violent bone in my body except the ones
in my fingers that wonder if the search results would be different
if I typed "How to Kill Yourself and Make Sure You Don't Come Back"
but then I'd probably get a "Zombie Apocalypse Survival Guide"
when surviving is the exact opposite of what I'm trying to do
(Drink my own urine? I don't think so!)
although perhaps the website would have tips on how to kill yourself
when all hope for humanity has withered and that's one of the reasons
I'm here in the first place but those people are loons
and probably got their tips from movies but I'm sort of a loon
because now I'm thinking about Googling "How to Kill Yourself
and Make Sure It Doesn't End up on Facebook" because I don't want
people saying I was a good person (I'm not) or acting like they never
saw it coming (they did) because the fact that I can predict
what people will say bores me and that's one of the reasons
I'm here in the first place.

i talk to my therapist in dreams

remember when i forgot how to remember
when my body when my body in defense
do you remember how i got that scar on
my thigh you know the one we don't speak about
when you know i could turn anything into art
anything if i could somehow offer my body
a sinecure my legs have forgotten their
purpose in defense of my arms of my breasts
funny how the thesaurus offers no synonyms
for breast but sometimes my frontal lobe topples
over with synonyms & ambulances shriek
in broca's area someone i don't remember
told me madness attacks your thoughts like a virus
simplified into binary code but aren't we nothing
but a summation of thoughts surrounded by twigs
& water show me how this is simple wake up

i had a sex dream

about my therapist
last night she argued
karen horney to me

said hello to my boy-
friend when he left
the church i was born in

wished my mind wasn't
frenetic so we could go
steady and she could keep

her job it was so sexy
the way she touched my
hair told me years ago they

would have beat me
stretched me between two
logs smeared honey on my

parts and waited for the bees
to come her words alone
made me cum

The Weave on 3rd Avenue

On my usual walk to class
there is this woman walking in front of me,
sun warping the bedazzled cross on her shirt.
All rail legs and cheekbones, she could be a model.
She is yapping on her phone to some guy
named Henry, presumably her significant other.
Poor, sweet Henry, forever waiting on the other
end for his chance to speak. I am just about to pass
this woman when a chunk of her hair hits the ground
in front of me. I think the mass looks like a tangled octopus.
Of course, it is not really this woman's hair, but a weave.
I watch her massage her scalp where the octopus once was,
completely silent, and I will Henry to use this as his chance
to speak. She considers picking it up off the ground
but immediately thinks better of it and keeps walking.
I wonder to myself if this is a statement about women
and how we go through some ridiculous shit to look pretty
but never want to admit to the world just how ridiculous it is,
or if this woman had dropped herself somewhere along the way
and was too embarrassed to get up. I was about to ask
her when she picked up where she left off, with
"Henry, are you even listening?"

Watching Ancient Aliens

Things you learned while I was in the shower:
Aliens killed the dinosaurs and gave Einstein
physics cheat sheets. It creeps you out because
it's on the History Channel. I laugh, collapse
on the pillow next to you, naked and wet.
We're drunk, and on vacation. Our motel is cheap,
but not cheap enough. It reeks of stale cigarettes,
and the TV only gets one channel. We are dumb
and defenseless.

I consider aliens, and a world with dissolving doors.
A sun that burns brighter as it sets, bleeding
through our curtains until we can't tell the difference
between fire and flowerbeds. I will imagine I'm
dreaming, waking the next morning wondering
how I never noticed your eyes were green,
chalking your strange words up to a bad hangover.

Giselle's Anxieties

Something terrible happens
inside of me
every time I change
the cat's water
or dump out her litter.
Even when I throw her
a treat, she looks up at me
with unmistakable fear.
Scared I'd thirst her to death
for the floaties in her dish,
terrified of her own secretions.
(Were they too much?
Would I leave her nowhere
to take future shits?)
Each morning, she waits
by the pill cabinet,
linking my vitamins
to her treats.
Each morning she runs
for them, distrusting
me even then, afraid
I'd renege on my offer,
pry them from her teeth,
decide she wasn't worthy
of those little luxuries
after all. I wish I could
talk to her like a daughter,
teach her unconditional love.
But maybe it's a good thing
she can't understand
because then she'd expect
more than I could give.

Our Cat Is a Feminist

Our cat often screams at 4 am.
You're a talented sleeper, so sometimes
it goes on for 3 or 4 hours before you roll
over to shush her, which only makes
her scream louder.

This is her telling you no man
will silence her. I tell you so one morning,
only half-joking. You roll your eyes
and say stop making everything
about feminism.

But how can anything not be about feminism
when it's us the birds keep interrupting
at 4 in the morning while you snore
and thrash in the steam of your sweat
like a car engine under stolen blankets?

My mother thinks I should go to law school

because I could never finish

a thought. At the time, I thought
she just wanted me to give up poetry
so I didn't have to work at call centers or restaurants
or feel the same dried-out quality she embodied
in her sagging shoulders each morning at the breakfast
table.

Women fought for your right to be a lawyer, she'd say.
You're a feminist. Don't you want to make more money
than your husband?

This was never the appropriate point in the conversation
to mention feminists don't need husbands, or that she doesn't

finish thoughts either. That she still watches court
shows on TV at night and voted Judge Judy
for president in our most recent election. That she takes
comfort in filing charts for ill patients and still calls
herself a nurse based on ancient knowledge,

though she hasn't used a needle in thirteen years.

Shopping for a Washing Machine

I think of my mother in the laundry room, spooning
scoop after scoop of Tide into the empty drum,
sometimes bringing the cap to her nose first like sniffing
a daisy. She scrubbed stubborn stains with blue Dawn
dish detergent. *Always the blue*, she'd say, demonstrating
on my grass-streaked cross-country shirt. *You'll
learn from your mistakes.* She'd count socks and panties,
making sure everything was accounted for before setting
the water level and checking tags for instructions.
We did our laundry on Sunday, and also had our family
meal. We weren't particularly holy, but sometimes my dad
didn't work that day. We were always running late, my mom fresh
from the shower in holey T-shirt and full face of makeup.
I'd help her peel potatoes, frantic to keep up with the flick
of her wrists, never quite getting there and often cutting
myself in the process. Again, my mom would fix my mistakes,
running cold water over the wound, sending diluted blood
swirling down the drain like that scene in *Psycho.*
We'd remember the laundry while putting down
silverware, now needing a second spin cycle to flatten
the wrinkles. So my mom would eat dinner
in her tattered shirt, the one with the cow, a souvenir
from that time she took my brother and I to a dairy
farm. On that day, we thought it was so funny,
but on those Sundays its goofy buck-tooth smile
seemed obscene. Sometimes my dad would
comment on something she could have done
better, and sometimes I agreed, but I had seen
her cry over the dishes enough times to know
better.

You think they're all the same, ready to buy
the first one you see for under $500, but I know
better. Washing machines are the one thing women
will always know better because everything in our lives
is about spinning and forgetting. I will make sure
we have the one with the steam cycle. I will never be late
for dinner. I will always look my best.

The News Will Be Our Unmaking

We face each other at the kitchen table,
my arms hugging my shins, your hands
running circles across your thighs.
We have long since given up conversation
about poetry or the weather, trading news
articles instead that glow up at us
from our phones. White men will take everything,
even my body. Even your union. Our coffees
grow cold and our cereal warm. I google your favorite
color and text it to you. You send back
an *I love you*. If either of us spoke,
our words would creak from disuse.
The world is our abortion. Outside
is our economy. Snow clings to the window,
obscuring our view.

Why You Need to Teach in Other States

I want to be somewhere water evaporates
before it hits the ground. Where I open every window,
even in winter. Or at least somewhere I have the choice.
A construction worker once told me fresh concrete smells
better in California. Perfume is more vivid. I want to live
somewhere with less mental illness. Dry heat to cure arthritis.
I'd even take wet heat to oil the rust of my creaking bones.
The ground needs to burn my feet, my unbreakable
skin. The air should be heavy enough to slow my racing
thoughts. Sea salt is nice, but not required. Outdoor bookstores,
poetry readings in the street. I can throw away ChapStick
and itchy sweaters. You wouldn't need to leave the house
if you didn't want to. I would shop for our groceries and learn
to love my heat-shocked hair. We wouldn't have to worry
about capsized cars or wind-strewn debris popping our snow
tires. The news boy would deliver the paper directly to our door
instead of throwing it out the window of his poorly heated van.
He may even ride a bicycle like they do in the movies. I read
a poem by a rural Pennsylvania poet today. I scoured the internet
for mention of the college she teaches at. No luck. If you think
about the weather, God will smite you. She knows how it is.
She's probably applying for the same jobs as you.
She doesn't want to jinx her chance.

Watching You Write before Work

Bare chest contrasting the dress
slacks with the stiff crease
that mimics your linear shin.
Hands shoved between
your starched thighs.
How can I sleep in? Your lips
curling around the words
stuck in the annals of your
mind. The way you stroke
your pen in the suggestive
way the pad of your finger
swirls around the outline
of my nipple under a thin
T-shirt. If I were the words,
I wouldn't be so shy to ink.

Feet Poem

I present them to you
no longer guarded
by socks. I cut
the word "cut"
into the insoles
to get your attention
but leave the arches
pearly, a gift
for your lips.
Toes ripe as plums,
you will want to drowse
on them. Praise
their perfect anatomy.
Devour them upon
waking, their scent
more potent than
the most robust coffee.
Their webbing flutters
for you. You will beg
to own them for yourself.
Venerate them. Anoint
them with your tongue.
Bind them from prying
eyes until they bloom
into lotus flowers.

Nude Beach

proof that you don't need anything
you can buy,

except for water.

we are surrounded by a body
of undrinkable water
& i'm thirsty

for you. i wanted to touch
you last night when it was cold
& again this morning at breakfast,

but the moment
was over
before my hand
could work up
the nerve.

here there's nothing
between us
& ourselves,
us & each other,

& our neighbors
& our skin folds
& the sand.

your air,
your sweat,
your sunscreen

belong to me now.
all morning,

the sun's had its way
with your thighs.

how red will you burn
when i have mine?

Sun King

His bosky limbs mean he doesn't need to kneel.
His back will hurt tomorrow. My knees will hurt

tomorrow. I kneel. You don't need pride to pull
weeds, but he manages it. Sweat carves out his muscles,

shines them like points on a crown. He is regal.
My face is red with sun, and arousal. I look up at him

and I am a wildflower at his feet. I am a weed
under his feet. He extends a gloved hand and I take it.

He lifts me up by my roots, steadies me with an arm.
My thank you stuffs up with love like a pebble trapped

in the tube of this ball point pen. He has me in awe.
I will always be in awe.

Sunburn

Dead skin cells
curl away from you
like old sheets
of papyrus,
crumbling like words
under a lighter.
I sit in your shadow.
Oblivious, you watch
the ocean,
hair lit like a leaf
on the first day
of autumn—
another mass
of cells made to dry
& break, sighing
under the rubber
of a stranger's
booted feet.
& I am nothing
but another
living thing
who knows what
hurts, yet can't
resist reaching
out and touching it.

the fire

it burned & it burned with a man & a woman
& a daughter & a daughter & a cat still inside

my mom woke us up to take us to our grandma's
a block away & my brother the fact machine even

at eight years old told me they'd suffocate from smoke
before the heat got to their organs so stop conjuring up

images of exploding fruit my mother dressed us
with every piece of clothing we owned & i asked

her how fires keep burning in the snow & she didn't
have an answer & it was so hot that night i wished

i wasn't wearing all those layers i made such a fuss
that my uncle modeled a miniature doll house for me

as a christmas present & it was the most beautiful
house on our block until the one day my brother took

a match to my barbie & then the house was vacant
& vacant houses aren't as beautiful everybody envied

their family which is why they made a parking lot
on the foundation & now children learn how to ride

their bikes on the concrete of their unmarked graves

The Witch

Her eyes make little boys give up their ice cream.
Salons pay good money to cut her hair.
A flash of her earlobe gets criminals talking faster than the FBI.
Her mouth makes the weather more interesting than politics.
Imagining the hollow of her throat is illegal in 7 states.
Her voice invented the opera.
Several constellations are named after her shoulders.
Her breasts started a war. Twice.
Her lungs are conch shells
and her breath is why it's so expensive to pitch an umbrella at the beach.
Her heart makes schoolgirls question their sexuality.
Her heart is an entrance sign.
In some circles even thinking about her heart is considered cheating.
GPS systems go kaput when her hands dispute their directions.
Her arms are worth more than all the wedding rings in the world.
Her stomach keeps men in the kitchen.
Her ovaries are hot enough to fry an egg on.
Her ass is the logic behind yoga pants.
Her hips are jungle gyms that are never too high to jump from.
Her thighs inspired the two-way street.
Her toes started underground fetish clubs.
Grown men build treehouses to peer into the mystery of her closet.
Her name is androgynous.
By the time you speak it aloud you're already damned.

her illness is

showering & never getting clean showering with her clothes on leaving wet clothes on the floor & relishing the smell of mold as it suits her her mom calling her love life the wounded animal project coming down on them like religion fucking like a pneumatic drill flatlining when they ask if she's close she is the consequence of using the sad girl for drunk sex on a bad first date keeping razors in her pocket to remind herself she could addiction to things she will never do memorizing her light switches in case she has a nightmare & her cat doesn't stir because he's sick of her shit constantly questioning the meaning of big bodies in little spaces & little bodies in big spaces preferring blowjobs to sex & never letting a man go down on her taking too many vitamins & supplements because she loves the word supplement because it means she might be able to change who she is spooning mood stabilizers from a stranger's hip bones too many doctors too many pills constipation unable to hold down a job tired tired tired & drinking too much water & gaining weight & losing weight faster than she can run finally dating someone her mom approves of & nicknaming him prime number & she still can't cum but he makes her want to try explaining to friends that the mess in her car is a metaphor for her life scratching the furniture feeling magical if she goes one day without crying forgetting to lock doors behind her referring to herself with a lowercase i thinking every word should be abbreviated but not knowing how right-clicking on her name with no thesaurus suggestions patiently waiting for someone to tell her everyone wants to kill themselves sometimes if only to reply but i've been wanting for ten years

www.ingramcontent.com/pod-product-compliance
Lightning Source LLC
Chambersburg PA
CBHW022012080426
42733CB00007B/570